100 HANDS-ON SCIENCE ACTIVITIES TO DO AT HOME

DISCOVER THE SCIENCE TO EVERY DAY LIFE

DR DHEERAJ MEHROTRA

Contents

Preface

Curiosity, exploration, and practical learning are at the heart of science, not rote memorisation of data from textbooks. Encouraging young minds to experiment, investigate, and experience science in a fun and interactive way, Hands-On Science Activities To Do At Home is sure to kindle their imaginations.

The scientific experiments in this book are perfect for kids since they are fun, easy, and safe to do at home with everyday household items. Experiments like generating slime, constructing a balloon rocket, or witnessing the power of static electricity are designed to assist young learners in understanding scientific principles via hands-on experiences. Other examples include crafting a handmade volcano.

The exercises in this book cover physics, chemistry, biology, and earth science. Each experiment includes detailed directions, explanations of scientific concepts, and examples of their practical applications to help students better grasp the material.

We believe science education should be an exciting journey that encourages exploration, analysis, and originality. This book can help make any home into a little laboratory where kids can playfully experiment, learn by doing, and ask plenty of questions.

We wish this book well for all involved in science education, especially parents, instructors, and young scientists. We hope it helps create a more engaging, relevant, and enjoyable learning environment. Join me as we explore the wonders of science, one thrilling experiment at a time!

Have fun trying new things!

www.authordheerajmehrotra.com

ONE

HANDS-ON SCIENCE ACTIVITIES TO DO AT HOME

Environmental Science Experiments

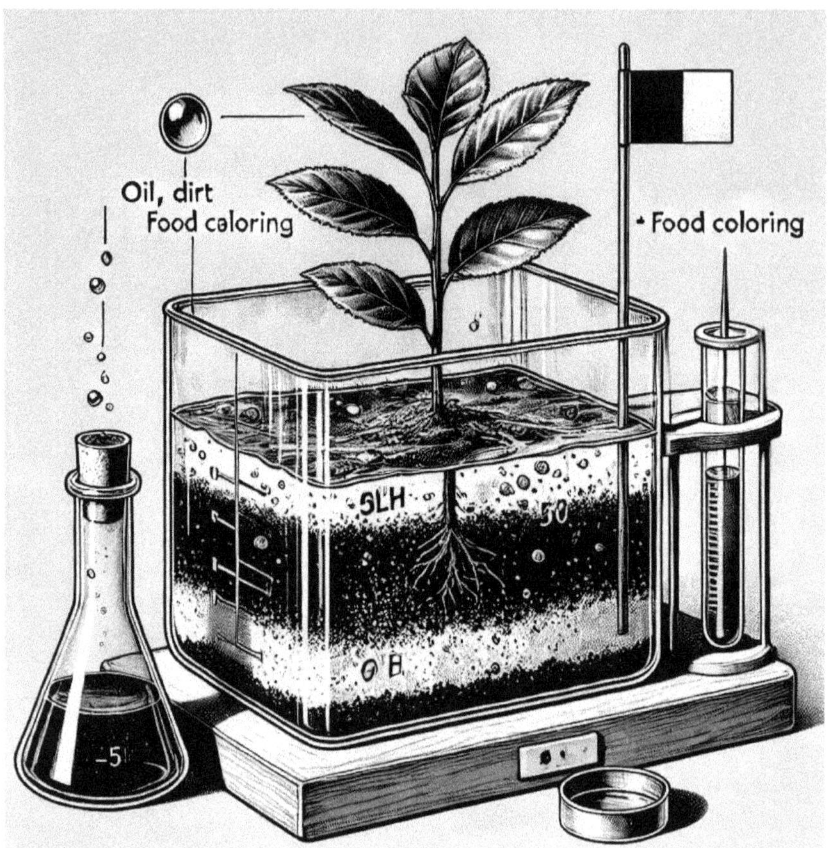

Pollution and Water:

Add oil, dirt, or food colouring to the water in a clear container. Observe how it affects clarity and plant growth.

Precaution: Use gloves and avoid spilling pollutants.

▷▷▷

Water Filter:

Layer sand, gravel, and charcoal in a plastic bottle. Pour dirty water through and observe filtration.

Precaution: Use clean materials and avoid drinking filtered water.

▷▷▷

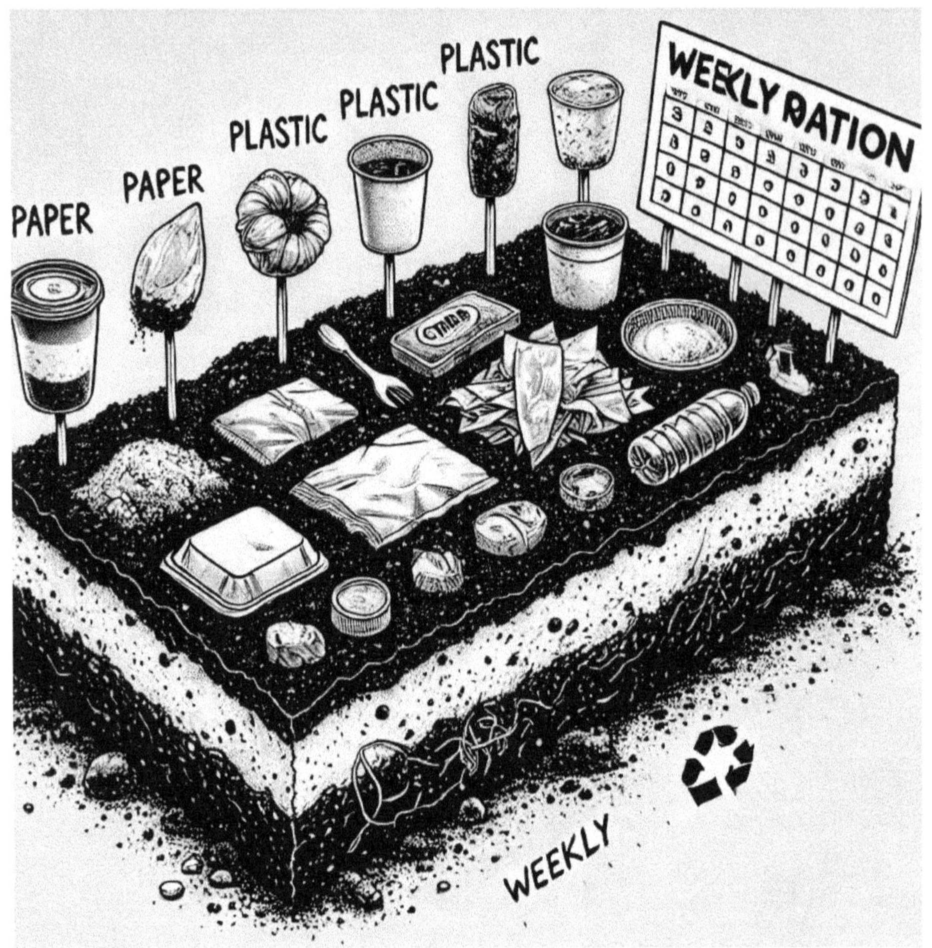

Decomposition:

Bury paper, plastic, and food in soil. Check weekly to see which decomposes fastest.

Precaution:

Wear gloves and wash hands after handling soil.

ⱣⱣⱣ

Solar Oven:

Line a box with foil, cover it with plastic wrap, and place food inside. Use sunlight to cook.

Precaution:

Avoid touching hot surfaces.

❧❧❧

Heat Insulation:

Wrap jars of hot water in foil, cloth, or paper. Measure temperature changes over time.

Precaution: Handle hot water carefully.

▷▷▷

ᐅᐅᐅ

Fun and Easy Experiments

ᐅᐅᐅ

Lava Lamp:

Fill a bottle with oil, water, and food colouring. Drop Alka-Seltzer tablets into the mixture to create bubbling "lava."

Precaution: Avoid ingestion and clean spills immediately.

ᗡᗡᗡ

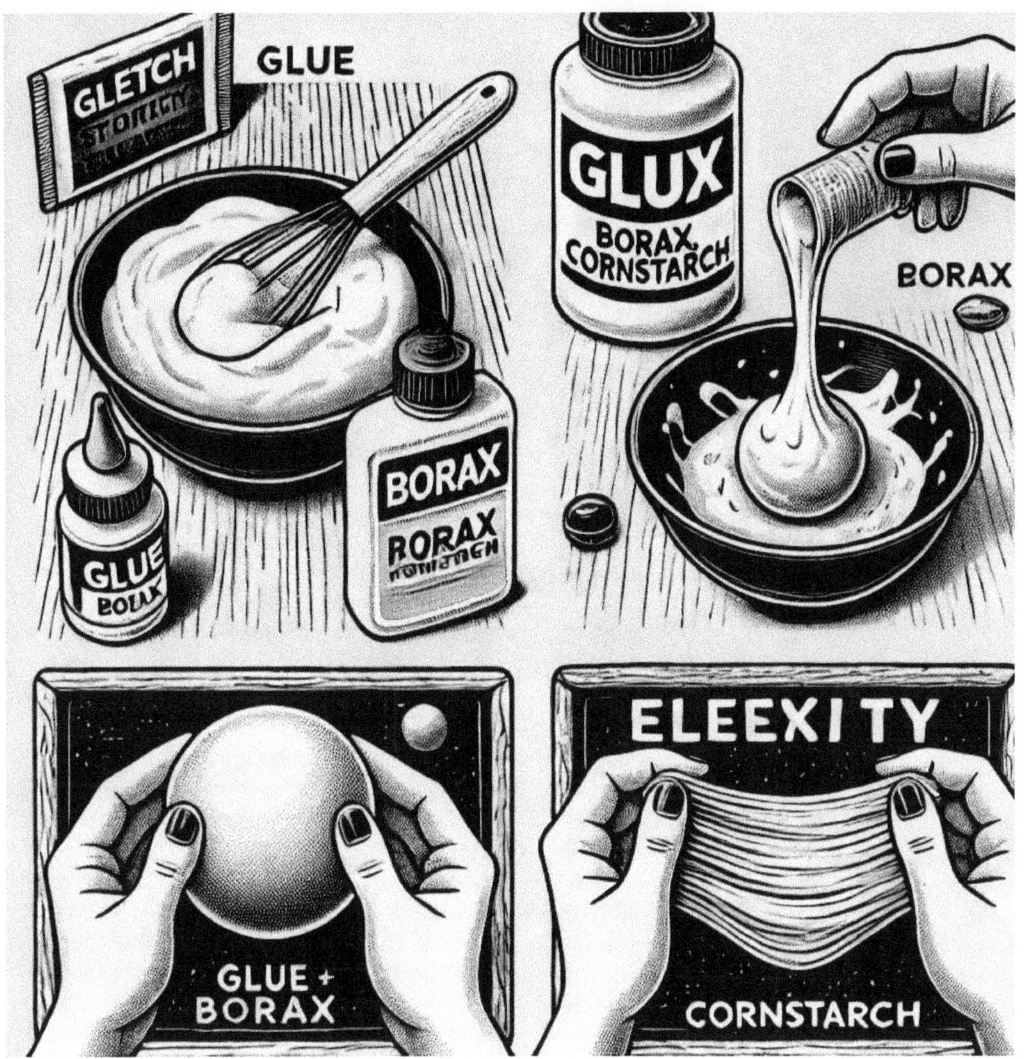

Bouncy Ball:

Mix glue, borax, and cornstarch to form a stretchy ball.

Precaution: Avoid contact with eyes and wash hands after handling.

▷▷▷

Kaleidoscope:

Use mirrors, beads, and a cardboard tube to create colourful patterns.

Precaution:

Be careful when handling mirrors to avoid cuts.

▷▷▷

Rainbow:

Shine a flashlight through a glass of water onto white paper to create a rainbow.

Precaution: Avoid spilling water near electrical devices.

⊳⊳⊳

Slingshot:

Use rubber bands and a small pouch to launch lightweight objects.

Precaution: Avoid aiming at people or fragile items.

ᐅᐅᐅ

Advanced Experiments

Homemade Robot:

Build a simple robot using a small motor, batteries, and craft materials.

Precaution:

Handle batteries carefully and avoid short circuits.

❦❦❦

Hovercraft:

Attach a balloon to a CD with a bottle cap. Inflate the balloon and watch it glide.

Precaution:

Use on smooth surfaces to avoid damage.

❯❯❯

Rocket:

Create a small rocket with a film canister, baking soda, and vinegar.

Precaution:

Launch outdoors and stand back.

ϷϷϷ

Solar-Powered Car:

Attach a small solar panel to a toy car. Test in sunlight.

Precaution:

Avoid overheating the solar panel.

ᐅᐅᐅ

Windmill:

Build blades from cardboard and attach them to a stick. Use a fan to simulate wind.

Precaution:

Ensure blades are securely connected.

❧❧❧

❧❧❧

Experiments with Light and Sound

❧❧❧

Rainbow Prism:

Shine a light through a prism to split it into colours.

Precaution:

Handle the prism carefully to avoid drops.

ᗡᗡᗡ

Light Bending:

Place a pencil in a glass of water. Observe how it appears bent.

Precaution:

Avoid breaking the glass.

ᐅᐅᐅ

Sound Travel:

Tap a spoon against a table while holding a string to your ear. Compare sounds.

Precaution:

Avoid loud noises near ears.

▷▷▷

Musical Instrument:

Use rubber bands and a box to create a simple guitar.

Precaution:

Stretch bands carefully to avoid snapping.

ÞÞÞ

ᐅᐅᐅ

Environmental Science Experiments

ᐅᐅᐅ

Wind Turbine:

Build blades from cardboard and attach them to a stick. Use a fan to simulate wind and generate motion.

Precaution:

Ensure blades are securely attached to avoid accidents.

Oil Spill Cleanup:

Pour oil into the water. Test materials like sponges, straws, or cotton to see which cleans best.

Precaution:

Wear gloves and avoid spilling oil.

▷▷▷

Rainforest Model:

Layer soil, plants, and water in a container. Cover with plastic to create humidity.

Precaution:

Keep the container in a stable place to avoid spills.

ᗡᗡᗡ

Air Quality Test:

Place Vaseline on index cards and leave them outside. Check after a week for dust and particles.

Precaution:

Avoid placing cards in high-traffic areas.

ᐅᐅᐅ

Greenhouse:

Build a small greenhouse with plastic wrap and observe how it traps heat for plant growth.

Precaution:

Avoid overheating plants by providing ventilation.

ᐯᐯᐯ

ꕤꕤꕤ

Fun and Easy Experiments

ꕤꕤꕤ

Marble Run:

Build a track with cardboard tubes and ramps for marbles to roll down.

Precaution:

Ensure the structure is stable to prevent collapse.

❧❧❧

Balloon Hovercraft:

Attach a balloon to a CD with a bottle cap. Inflate the balloon and watch it hover.

Precaution:

Use on smooth surfaces to avoid damage.

ppp

Pinwheel:

Cut and fold paper into a pinwheel shape. Blow on it or place it in the wind to spin.

Precaution:

Avoid sharp edges when cutting paper.

ᗧᗧᗧ

Spinning Top:

Use a pencil and cardboard to create a top. Spin it to see how long it stays upright.

Precaution:

Ensure the top is balanced for smooth spinning.

ᐅᐅᐅ

Water Clock:

Poke a hole in a plastic bottle. Fill it with water and measure how long it takes to empty.

Precaution:

Place the bottle on a stable surface to avoid spills.

ᐅᐅᐅ

ᐅᐅᐅ

Advanced Experiments

ᐅᐅᐅ

Water Wheel:

Use plastic spoons and a bottle to create a wheel. Pour water over it to make it spin.

Precaution:

Ensure the wheel is securely attached to avoid accidents.

ᗡᗡᗡ

Hydroelectric Generator:

A water wheel and a small motor generate electricity from flowing water.

Precaution:

Avoid contact with water and electrical components.

❧❧❧

Electromagnet:

Wrap a nail with copper wire and connect it to a battery. Use it to pick up small metal objects.

Precaution:

Before use, disconnect the battery to avoid overheating the wire.

⊳⊳⊳

Battery:

Use lemons, nails, and copper coins to create a simple battery.

Precaution:

Avoid short circuits and handle nails carefully.

ᗡᗡᗡ

Radio:

Build a simple crystal radio using a coil, diode, and earphone.

Precaution:

Handle small components carefully to avoid injury.

▷▷▷

ϷϷϷ

Experiments with Light and Sound

ϷϷϷ

Light Reflection:

Shine a flashlight on mirrors and other surfaces to see how light reflects.

Precaution:

Avoid shining light directly into the eyes.

ᗡᗡᗡ

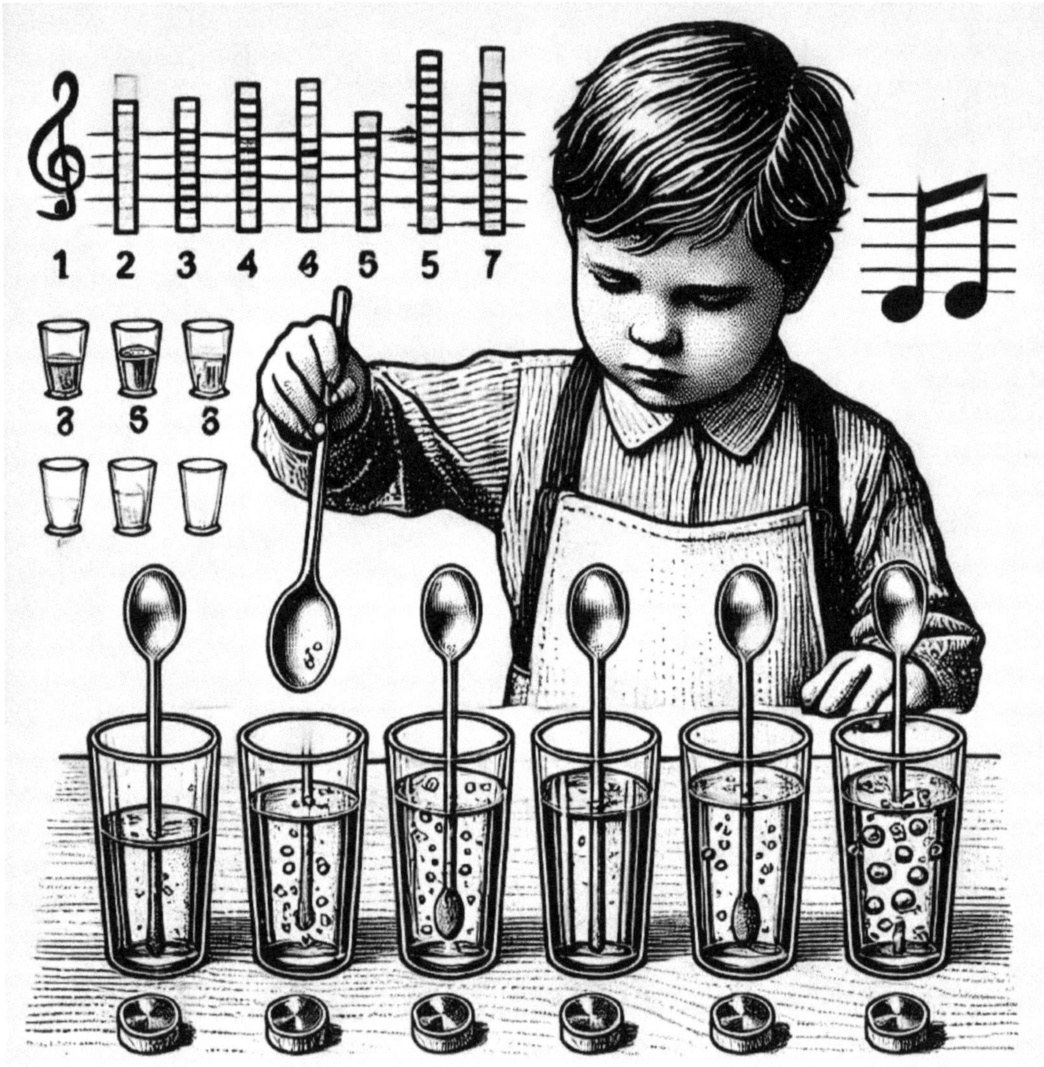

Sound Pitch:

Fill glasses with different amounts of water. Tap them to hear different pitches.

Precaution:

Avoid using fragile glassware.

Light and Plants:

Grow plants under different coloured lights to see how light affects growth.

Precaution:

Avoid overheating plants with excessive light.

❧❧❧

TWO

TOP 50 AI TOOLS TO EXPLORE ONLINE EXPERIMENTS

AI Tools for Education & Learning

ChatGPT – AI-powered conversational assistant for learning.

Google Bard – AI-based research and summarization tool.

Socratic by Google – AI tutor for students with step-by-step explanations.

Khanmigo (Khan Academy) – AI-assisted tutoring tool.

QuillBot – AI-powered paraphrasing and summarization tool.

Grammarly – AI tool for grammar and writing improvement.

Diffit – AI-powered lesson differentiation tool for teachers.

Quizlet AI – AI-generated study sets and quizzes.

Knowji – AI-based vocabulary learning platform.

TutorAI – AI-assisted personalized learning and tutoring.

AI Tools for Online Coding & Development

GitHub Copilot – AI-based coding assistant for developers.

Replit Ghostwriter – AI-powered coding and debugging assistant.

OpenAI Codex – AI model for generating and completing code.

CodeT5 – AI-based autocomplete tool for programmers.

Tabnine – AI-driven code suggestion tool.

DeepCode – AI-based code review and analysis tool.

SourceAI – AI-powered code generator.

JSXGraph – AI-based interactive mathematical visualization tool.

Codeium – AI-driven autocomplete for coding.

MutableAI – AI that accelerates software development.

AI Tools for Creativity & Design

DALL·E 3 – AI image generation from text descriptions.

Canva AI – AI-powered design assistance tool.

Runway ML – AI-based video and image editing platform.

Lumen5 – AI-driven video creation from text.

Deep Dream Generator – AI-powered artistic image transformation.

Artbreeder – AI-assisted image generation and modification.

This Person Does Not Exist – AI-generated realistic human faces.

Remove.bg – AI tool for removing image backgrounds.

Let's Enhance – AI-driven image upscaling and enhancement.

Veed.io – AI-powered video editing and captioning tool.

AI Tools for Scientific Research & Analysis

Elicit – AI research assistant for literature review.

Semantic Scholar – AI-powered research paper search engine.

Scite.ai – AI-driven citation analysis tool.

Consensus – AI tool for summarizing research papers.

ChatPDF – AI assistant for summarizing and analyzing PDFs.

IBM Watson Discovery – AI-powered data insights for research.

SciSpace Copilot – AI-based research assistant.

Perplexity AI – AI-powered contextual search engine.

Research Rabbit – AI-assisted literature exploration tool.

Litmaps – AI-driven research mapping tool.

AI Tools for Automation & Productivity

Zapier AI – AI-based workflow automation tool.

Notion AI – AI-powered content creation and management tool.

Taskade AI – AI-assisted task and project management.

Tome AI – AI-powered storytelling and presentation creation.

Copy.ai – AI-driven content generation.

Writesonic – AI-based content writing assistant.

Otter.ai – AI-powered transcription tool.

Speechify – AI text-to-speech reader.

Synthesia – AI-based video creation with avatars.

Descript – AI-driven podcast and video editing tool.

These tools cover education, research, coding, automation, creativity, and productivity, making them essential AI-powered resources for online experiments and exploration. ??

THREE
BOOKS BY THE SAME AUTHOR

Scan Here
FOR QUALITY BOOKS
For Home Library for
Parents, Educators &Students